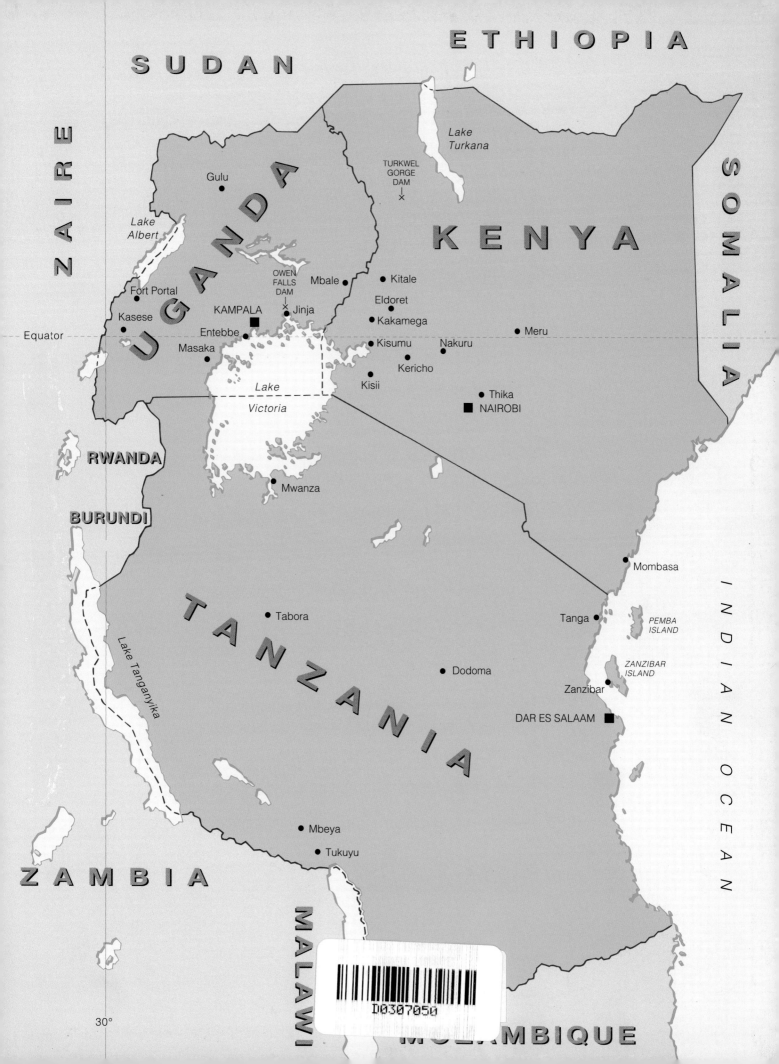

Kenya

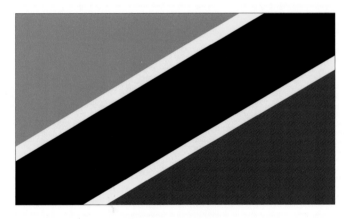

Tanzania

Uganda

WORLD FACT FILES

East Africa

Rob Bowden and Tony Binns

MACDONALD YOUNG BOOKS

First published in 1998 by Macdonald Young Books
An imprint of Wayland Publishers Ltd
© Macdonald Young Books 1998

Macdonald Young Books
61 Western Road
Hove
East Sussex
BN3 1JD

Find Macdonald Young Books on the Internet at
http://www.wayland.co.uk

Design and typesetting Roger Kohn Designs
Commissioning editor Hazel Songhurst
Editor Merle Thompson
Assistant editor Diana Russell
Picture research Paula Chapman
Maps János Márffy

We are grateful to the following for permission
to reproduce photographs:
Front Cover: Panos *above* (Sean Sprague);
Getty Images *below* (Daryl Balfour);
Axiom, pages 9 (Jim Holmes), 17 (Jim Holmes), 25 (Jim
Holmes), 45 *right* (Jim Holmes); Tony Binns, pages 18 *above*
and *below*, 19 *above*, 24 *below*, 33; B Coleman, pages 16
(Paul van Gaalen), 36 (Andy Purcell), 40 a*bove* (Christer
Fredriksson); Eye Ubiquitous, page 43 *above* (Thelma
Sanders); Getty Images, pages 10 (Rene Lynn), 12 (Nicholas
Parfitt); Robert Harding, pages 8 *below*, 11 (N A Callow), 31;
Hutchinson, pages 13 *below* (Patricio Goycolea), 41 (Crispin
Hughes); Images of Africa, pages 8 *above* (David Keith Jones),
15 (David Keith Jones), 28 (David Keith Jones), 29 (Peter
Tilbury), 39 *above* (David Keith Jones); Impact, pages 13
above (Javed A Jafferji), 14 (Javed A Jafferji), 30 *above*
(Javed A Jafferji), 30 *below* (Piers Cavendish), 34 (Jorn
Stjerneklar), 35 (Caroline Penn), 37 *above* and *below* (Piers
Cavendish), 40 *below*; Panos, pages 20 (Betty Press), 21
(Sean Sprague), 23 (Jeremy Hartley), 24 *above* (S Hackett),
32 (Trygve Bølstad), 39 *below* (Sean Sprague), 43 *below*,
(Sean Sprague), 44 (Crispin Hughes), 45 *left* (Liba Taylor);
Popperfoto, page 27; WPL, pages 22, 38.

The statistics given in this book are the most up to date
available at the time of going to press

Printed in Hong Kong by Wing King Tong

A CIP catalogue record for this book is available from
the British Library

ISBN: 0 7500 2435 6

CONTENTS

Words that are explained in the glossary are printed in
SMALL CAPITALS the first time they are mentioned in the text.

INTRODUCTION

East Africa includes three countries – Kenya, Tanzania and Uganda – covering a total area of 1,763,780 square kilometres: seven times bigger than the UK and almost one-fifth the size of the USA. In 1995, the region's population was nearly 80 million. As well as various African ethnic groups, this included people of European, Arabic and Asian origin – a legacy of the area's colonial past. East Africa has a very long history of human settlement. It has often been called 'The Cradle of Humankind', as the world's most ancient human remains have been found here.

The Great Rift Valley dominates East Africa and incorporates many spectacular features, such as Lake Victoria, the mountains of Kilimanjaro and Mount Kenya, and the soda lakes Nakuru and Natron with their masses of pink flamingoes. Wildlife is abundant throughout much of the region, and vast areas of land are dominated by millions of wildebeest, zebra and antelope.

Nairobi, Mombasa, Dar es Salaam and Kampala are thriving modern cities, in stark contrast to the vast SAVANNA plains of Tanzania, the rainforests of western Uganda, or the remote deserts of northern Kenya. These cities reflect East Africa's relatively advanced development levels compared with other African countries, but most of the region is very poor. Many rural people, such as the NOMADIC Turkana, face a daily struggle to survive.

◀ *The skull of 'Nutcracker Man' was discovered in northern Tanzania in 1959. At around 2 million years old, it is among the world's oldest known human remains.*

▼ *Nairobi, seen here from across Uhuru (freedom) Park, is East Africa's biggest city and one of the most important cities in the African continent.*

East Africa can be summarized as an area full of contrasts. Within its three countries, you will find almost anything you might imagine about the continent of Africa as a whole. This book explores the region, looking at its people, places and policies, and suggesting what its future direction and opportunities may be.

- Total area: 1,763,780 square kilometres
- Total population (1995): 79.3 million
- Population density: Average of 45 people per square kilometre (31 per square kilometre in Tanzania; 49 in Kenya; 90 in Uganda)
- Largest cities: Nairobi 1,500,000; Dar es Salaam 1,360,000; Kampala 773,000; Mombasa 465,000
- Highest mountain: Kilimanjaro (Tanzania), 5,895 metres
- Largest lake: Victoria, 69,500 square kilometres
- Official languages: Swahili, English, African languages
- Major religions: Christianity, Islam, traditional African beliefs
- Economy: Mainly agricultural and services (chiefly tourism)
- Major resources: Land, water, wildlife, gold, tin, copper
- Major products: Coffee, tea, cotton, fruit and vegetables
- Environmental problems: Water shortages, soil erosion, deforestation, DESERTIFICATION, urban pollution

 A Hindu temple in Kampala, Uganda, is evidence of the significant Asian population living in East Africa.

THE LANDSCAPE

▲ Mount Kilimanjaro, the highest peak in Africa, rises impressively out of the scenic Amboseli National Park that surrounds it.

East Africa is bordered by a total of nine countries, including Mozambique, Rwanda, Zaire and Somalia. Uganda is land-locked, while Kenya and Tanzania both have an eastern coastline on the Indian Ocean. Tanzania's territory includes the small islands of Pemba and Zanzibar, which lie just off the coast.

The landscape in East Africa is dominated by the Great Rift Valley, an enormous GEOLOGICAL FAULT stretching 6,400 kilometres from Jordan in the Middle East to Mozambique in southern Africa. The Rift Valley was created by massive earth movements over millions of years, twisting and buckling the surface to cause some

sections of land to rise and others to sink. The mountains, cliffs, valleys and soda lakes that result from such movements can be found along the whole length of the fault, but those in East Africa provide some of the most impressive scenery in the world.

There are several mountains in East Africa, including Africa's highest, Mount Kilimanjaro (5,895 metres). It rises from the plains on the border of Kenya and Tanzania, and its distinctive domed, snow-capped

summit is visible from hundreds of kilometres away. Other peaks include Mount Kenya (5,199 metres), Mount Elgon (4,321 metres) and the Ruwenzori range in western Uganda (rising to 5,119 metres).

The Ruwenzori Mountains, also known as the 'Mountains of the Moon', are particularly special because many rare plants and animals can be found in the tropical forests that cover their slopes. The forests extend westwards across the border into Zaire to form part of the massive Congo Basin, which covers more than 4.1 million square kilometres and includes the largest remaining area of tropical forest in Africa.

Africa's largest lake, Lake Victoria, straddles the borders between Kenya,

▶ *Tropical forests, known as 'montane forest', cling to the slopes of Mount Kenya National Park.*

KEY FACTS

● Zanzibar is the largest coral island off the African coast, covering 1,650 square kilometres.

● At 69,500 square kilometres, Lake Victoria is the world's second largest freshwater lake, after Lake Superior (82,400 square kilometres) in the USA/Canada.

● Ngorongoro, an extinct volcanic crater in northern Tanzania, is the second largest crater in the world.

Tanzania and Uganda. The lake is the starting point of the White Nile, which flows north through Uganda and into Sudan, joining the Blue Nile at Khartoum before flowing through Egypt to the Mediterranean. The region's other major rivers are the Tana and Galana in Kenya and the Rufiji and Njombe in Tanzania, which all flow eastwards to the Indian Ocean.

Other lakes in the region include Lake Turkana in northern Kenya, Lake Tanganyika on the Tanzania/Zaire border, and several soda lakes such as Lakes Nakuru and Bogoria in Kenya and Lake Natron in Tanzania. These soda lakes are formed because the high temperatures in

▲ *Savanna covers much of the East African landscape and is home to most of the region's abundant wildlife.*

the region cause much of the water to evaporate, leaving salt deposits behind which make the water more alkaline than in normal lakes. Few animals can live in such salty water, but one bird that has adapted very well is the flamingo. They can be seen on the lakes in their millions, especially at Lake Nakuru.

East Africa's 1,300 kilometres of coastline is among the finest in the world. It includes an almost continuous belt of coral reefs that provide an important habitat for fish and other marine life. The white sand beaches and tropical vegetation also make the coast an attractive tourist destination, with hundreds of thousands visiting every year.

The vast expanses of savanna grassland that cover much of the rest of East Africa are home to many of the region's people and most of its rich wildlife. Areas of savanna such as the Serengeti and the Maasai Mara contain some of the greatest concentrations of wildlife in the world. In northern Kenya, the savanna turns into a SEMI-ARID landscape where few people live and very little grows.

▲ *The white sands and clear blue sea of Zanzibar's coastline make it a popular tourist destination.*

▶ *The edges of the Great Rift Valley form steep slopes like these, which are called 'escarpments'. The valley can be seen stretching into the distance.*

CLIMATE AND WEATHER

The climate and weather in East Africa are as varied as its landscape. It is generally warm throughout the year, with temperatures ranging from 10°C to 40°C. The coastal strip and the low valley areas are normally the hottest parts of the region, while the highland plains (such as those around Nairobi) are noticeably cooler. The mountainous areas are also much cooler; several of the highest are snow-capped throughout the year, even though they are almost on the Equator. Mount Kilimanjaro is so cold at the top that it even has glaciers. By contrast, the far north of the region is extremely hot for much of the year – temperatures of 45°C are common near Lake Turkana in northern Kenya.

Rainfall is the most important element in the local climate. It arrives in two distinct seasons: the main or 'long' rains between March and May, and the secondary or 'short' rains between October and December. At the peak of the rains in April, there are often violent storms and 300–400 mm may fall in a single month – more than half of London's annual total. Life in East Africa depends on the rains; the amount that falls can mean the difference between life and

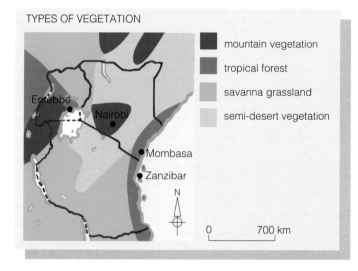

TYPES OF VEGETATION

- mountain vegetation
- tropical forest
- savanna grassland
- semi-desert vegetation

Entebbe
Nairobi
Mombasa
Zanzibar
N
0   700 km

KEY FACTS

● Kampala, the Ugandan capital, has thunderstorms on more than 200 days in an average year.
● The region around Kericho in western Kenya has hailstorms on more than 100 days a year – one of the highest rates in the world.
● Tukuyu on Lake Malawi in Tanzania has recorded rainfall of 432 mm in a single day – more than would normally fall in a month during the wet season.

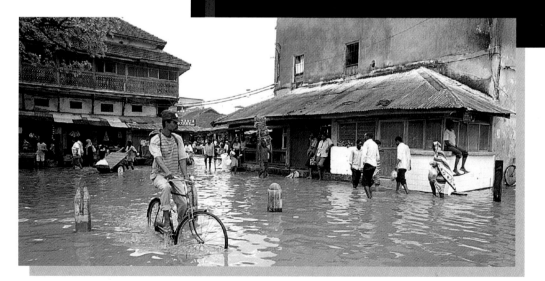

▶ **During the rainy season, short and violent storms can often lead to serious flooding, as in this Zanzibar street. However, local people are used to this and just carry on with their daily lives.**

death, both for the region's people and for its animals.

In the dry season, strong swirling winds create whirlwinds, or 'dust devils', that can be seen racing across the plains, sometimes from several kilometres away. In the far north of Kenya, rainfall is so sparse that the people there have adopted a nomadic lifestyle. They may have to travel a long way on foot to find water and

▲ *Even though it stands just south of the Equator, the top of Mount Kilimanjaro is so cold that it has permanent glaciers.*

pasture for themselves and their animals. The extreme heat across much of East Africa means that water collected in lakes and rivers during the rains quickly evaporates. In some years, even quite large lakes can dry up completely.

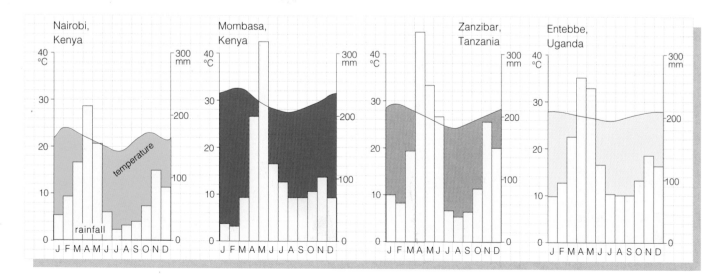

NATURAL RESOURCES

East Africa has relatively few natural resources compared with southern or western Africa, and very few compared with the UK and USA. There are limited deposits of metals such as gold in Kenya and Tanzania, copper in Uganda and tin in Tanzania, but nothing very significant in relation to world production figures. For example, Tanzania produced only 5 tonnes of tin in 1994, which places it outside the top 20 world producers. Similarly, the region does have precious and semi-precious stones, including diamonds, rubies and garnets, but nowhere near the quantity found in southern Africa.

East Africa's greatest resources are its land and wildlife. The land is intensively cultivated to produce CASH CROPS such as coffee, tea, cotton and fruit and vegetable products, while the wildlife helps attract thousands of tourists, who bring valuable foreign currency to the region.

Most of the rural areas lack any form of electricity, so people meet their energy needs by collecting wood for burning. This can often take a long time and may involve walking great distances just to get enough timber to last for a few days. The process can also be damaging to the environment if wood is taken more quickly than the trees can re-grow.

In the cities and towns, electricity is generated from imported oil or from hydro-

▼ *Wildlife is one of East Africa's key resources, attracting visitors from all over the world to places such as the Maasai Mara in Kenya.*

► *Fuelwood is a vital source of energy and people may walk far to collect it. They carry it home on their heads – this is called 'head-loading'.*

KEY FACTS

● In 1994, Kenya produced 20 kg of gold, a tiny slice of total world production of more than 2 million kilograms.

● 70–80% of the region's population rely on fuelwood for cooking, heating and lighting.

● The Turkwel Gorge hydro-electric dam was built by the French in 1990. It now produces 105 megawatts of electricity a year: about 20% of Kenya's total needs in 1997.

● Kenya's Olkaria geothermal power station, opened in 1981, produces 45 megawatts of electricity a year from three generators.

KEY NATURAL RESOURCES

KENYA	TANZANIA	UGANDA
gold	tin	copper
limestone	phosphates	cobalt
soda ash	iron ore	limestone
salt barytes	coal	salt
rubies	diamonds	wildlife
fluorspar	gemstones	
garnets	gold	
wildlife	natural gas	
	nickel	
	wildlife	

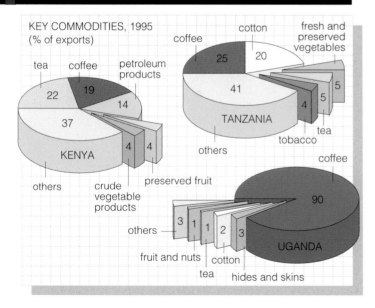

KEY COMMODITIES, 1995 (% of exports)

KENYA: tea 22, coffee 19, petroleum products 14, crude vegetable products 4, preserved fruit 4, others 37

TANZANIA: coffee 25, cotton 20, fresh and preserved vegetables 5, tea 5, tobacco 4, others 41

UGANDA: coffee 90, cotton 3, tea 2, hides and skins 1, fruit and nuts 1, others 3

electricity plants such as the Owen Falls Dam on Lake Victoria in Uganda and the Turkwel Gorge Dam in northern Kenya. A small amount of electricity is produced by using the heat of the volcanic earth at Olkaria, near Nakuru in central Kenya, a technique known as geothermal power. Some factories even produce electricity by burning crop waste. For example, a sugar-cane factory near Kakamega in western Kenya meets its electricity needs by burning the waste cane (bagasse) after the sugar has been squeezed from it.

17

POPULATION

The population of East Africa is among the fastest growing in the world, rising at an average of 3% per year – compared with 1% in the USA or just 0.4% in the UK. At this rate, the region's 1995 population of 80 million will increase to reach more than 110 million in the year 2005, rising to nearly 200 million by 2025.

URBANIZATION

The cities are growing particularly fast, as overcrowding in rural areas forces people to move to urban centres in search of work, a process called 'rural–urban migration'. The towns and cities cannot grow fast enough to cope with the migration, and around most large centres people have started building their own homes out of basic materials. These 'shanty towns' are often very crowded, with no fresh water or sanitation facilities. Some, like Mathare just outside Nairobi, are built in valleys, so that when the rains arrive they are often flooded and people may lose all their possessions.

▲ *Like other large cities, Nairobi attracts people from the rural areas who hope to find jobs and homes.*

▼ *Shanty towns, such as this one in Mathare Valley outside Nairobi, have grown rapidly to house the large numbers of people who are moving into urban areas.*

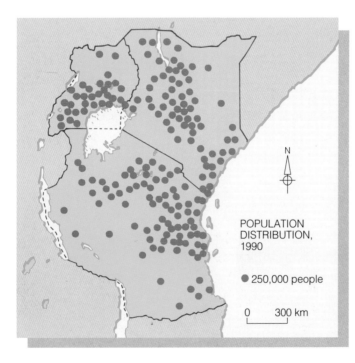

POPULATION
DISTRIBUTION,
1990

● 250,000 people

0   300 km

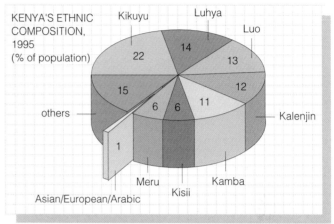

◀ *One of the smaller tribal groups, the Pokot people live in north-western Kenya. These young women are in traditional dress to go to market.*

KENYA'S ETHNIC COMPOSITION, 1995 (% of population)

Kikuyu 22
Luhya 14
Luo 13
Kalenjin 12
Kamba 11
Kisii 6
Meru 6
others 15
Asian/European/Arabic 1

ETHNIC GROUPS

The vast majority of the population is African, but they are broken down into several different ethnic groups, or 'tribes'. In Kenya alone there are over 70 such groups, each with their own language and lifestyle. In the region as a whole, people can be split into two main groups: the Bantu and the Nilotic people. The Bantu are farmers, originally from western Africa, and include the Kikuyu in Kenya, the WaSukumu in Tanzania and the Buganda in Uganda. The Nilotic people came from the Nile Valley area and are mainly PASTORALISTS. They include the Lango in Uganda, the Luo in Kenya and the Maasai, who live all over the region.

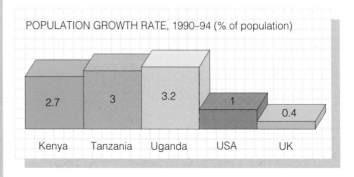

POPULATION GROWTH RATE, 1990–94 (% of population)

Kenya	Tanzania	Uganda	USA	UK
2.7	3	3.2	1	0.4

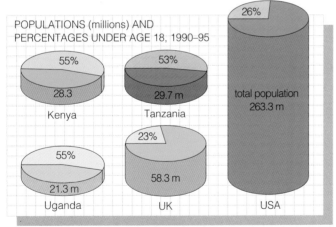

POPULATIONS (millions) AND
PERCENTAGES UNDER AGE 18, 1990–95

Kenya 55% / 28.3

Tanzania 53% / 29.7 m

Uganda 55% / 21.3 m

UK 23% / 58.3 m

USA 26% / total population 263.3 m

Several of the tribal groups still fight each other over the ownership of traditional lands and animals, but these are normally small, local disputes – rather than the major civil wars that neighbouring African countries such as Zaire and Mozambique have witnessed in recent years.

▲ *More than half the population of East Africa are children. Here in a Nairobi housing estate, a group of boys are playing with toy cars and buses that they have made themselves out of bits of scrap material.*

MINORITY GROUPS

East Africa's history of colonial rule brought other groups to the region too. Arabic people live along the coastline, descendants of slave traders who once ruled that area. Their main city was Mombasa in Kenya, where the Arab influence can be seen in the architecture today. The island of Zanzibar off the Tanzanian coast is still mainly inhabited by Arabic people.

Europeans colonized East Africa around 100 years ago, with the Germans ruling

KEY FACTS

● East Africa's population growth rate is 3 times faster than in the USA and more than 7 times faster than in the UK.

● In 1960, only 5% of Tanzania's population lived in towns and cities. In 1995, the figure was 24%.

● In 1950, 39% of Kenya's population was under the age of 14. By 1990, the figure had risen to 50%: the same as in Uganda and 1% more than in Tanzania.

● In 1995, there were more than 240,000 refugees in Kenya – about 200,000 of them from neighbouring Somalia.

▶ **AIDS *is a major threat to the region's population. There are major efforts in all three countries to make people aware of the dangers of the disease.***

what is now Tanzania and the British controlling Kenya and Uganda. After the First World War, Tanzania also became British and Britain ruled the whole region until the early 1960s, when it gained INDEPENDENCE. Many Europeans still live in East Africa, either in the cities or on large farms and plantations. There are also many people of Asian descent in Kenya and Uganda, whose ancestors arrived during British rule mainly to work on the Mombasa–Uganda railway. Kisumu, on the north-east shore of Lake Victoria, has a particularly high Asian population.

CURRENT ISSUES

Over 50% of East Africa's population is under 18 years old – more than double the proportion in most of Europe and North America. It is a challenge to provide schools, jobs and homes for so many young people. And the rapidly growing population will continue to pose such problems, as today's children marry and have children of their own.

One of the major problems facing the population today is that of AIDS. East Africa has one of the world's highest rates of HIV infection (which leads to AIDS). The infection rate is especially high in urban areas. Governments and other organizations are working very hard to educate people about the dangers of AIDS, and posters reminding people of the risks can be seen throughout the region.

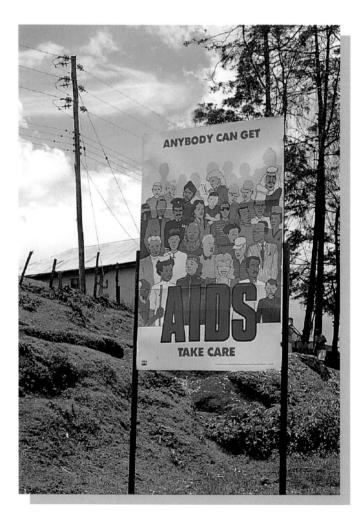

DAILY LIFE

Life is very hard for most of East Africa's people, who work long hours for little reward. Disease and malnutrition are also constant threats. Life expectancy has been slowly increasing over the past 20 years, but is still only 55 years in Kenya and just 44 in Uganda – more than 30 years less than in the UK or USA and significantly less than in other developing countries such as India (62) or Brazil (67). Infant mortality is also still high, with one in ten children in Tanzania and Uganda dying before their first birthday.

These figures are averages. The quality of people's daily lives is actually very different, depending on whether they live in urban or rural areas.

INFANT MORTALITY, 1995
(deaths under 1 year old per 1,000)

6	UK
8	USA
27	Russia
61	Kenya
100	Tanzania
111	Uganda
191	Niger
4	Finland
4	Japan
4	Sweden

LIFE EXPECTANCY AT BIRTH,
1995 (years)

55	Kenya
52	Tanzania
44	Uganda
67	Brazil
80	Japan
77	UK
76	USA

◀ *For better-paid workers, such as this Asian family in Mombasa, Kenya, daily life is similar to that in western Europe or the USA. Their apartment has fresh water, proper toilets, and electricity for lighting and modern appliances.*

URBAN LIFE

People in towns work in offices, banks, shops, factories and restaurants in much the same way as people in European or US cities. Many people also work in the INFORMAL SECTOR. Such jobs include polishing shoes, vending newspapers and magazines, washing windscreens, selling fruit and vegetables on the street or in a market, cleaning and begging. As the urban population grows at about twice the national rate, the informal sector is expanding. If the

URBAN POPULATION GROWTH, 1990–94 (% of population)

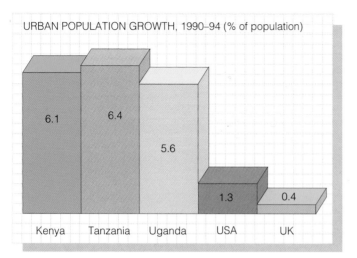

Kenya	Tanzania	Uganda	USA	UK
6.1	6.4	5.6	1.3	0.4

RURAL LIFE

Almost 80% of people in East Africa still live in rural areas, and for them daily life is very different. Many of them live in small villages and have farms nearby where they grow food to feed their families and a little extra to sell. The whole family, which may include six or seven children, are involved in the farm and they often work from the minute the sun rises to the minute it sets. Some people may find paid work on large plantation farms, such as the tea estates

▲ *A fruit and vegetable market at Kakamega, Kenya. These women may have travelled a long way by bus, or on foot, to sell their produce.*

population continues to increase so rapidly, unemployment in the urban areas is bound to increase.

Better-paid workers live in apartments or in homes in the suburbs, but most live in shanty towns on the edge of urban areas or in villages some distance away, commuting into the centre every day by public transport. Few people earn enough to own a car; instead, they rely on public buses and on private minibuses or vans, known as MATATUS, that cover most of the main routes. Many of these vehicles are packed to overflowing, with passengers hanging out of the windows and doors.

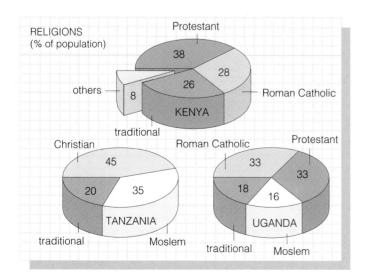

RELIGIONS
(% of population)

KENYA
- Protestant 38
- Roman Catholic 28
- traditional 26
- others 8

TANZANIA
- Christian 45
- Moslem 35
- traditional 20

UGANDA
- Protestant 33
- Roman Catholic 33
- Moslem 16
- traditional 18

◀ *Women and girls have to work particularly hard in rural areas. Here, three girls are pounding maize to make flour.*

▶ *Rural children are lucky if they go to school. Even if they do, the schools often lack basic items such as desks, books and paper.*

near Kericho in south-western Kenya. In other areas, they may grow crops to sell to larger farmers and factories, who will then export them.

People are generally much poorer in the rural areas, living in very basic homes with

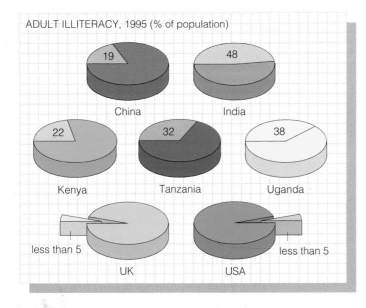

ADULT ILLITERACY, 1995 (% of population)

19	48
China	India

22	32	38
Kenya	Tanzania	Uganda

less than 5	less than 5
UK	USA

▲ *People may use local resources to make furniture or crafts to sell in urban markets. These men near Lake Victoria are making chairs from papyrus reeds.*

EDUCATION

Education in rural areas is very poor. Children must help on the family farm or in the home; in parts of Kenya less than half of them enrol in school, compared with a national average of 90%. Primary education is free, but families have to find money for books, uniforms and stationery. Many parents can only afford to send one or two of their children to school, and it is usually the girls who stay at home. This means that more than 30% of the adult population in East Africa cannot read or write. In some very rural areas, the figure may be as high as 70% among women.

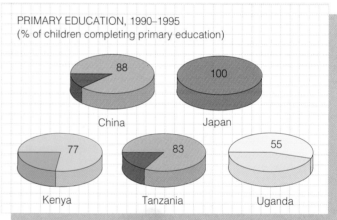

PRIMARY EDUCATION, 1990–1995
(% of children completing primary education)

88 China
100 Japan
77 Kenya
83 Tanzania
55 Uganda

no electricity or services. They have to spend many hours collecting wood for cooking and water for drinking. Some people make items such as cane furniture, carvings and baskets to try to earn a little extra money, but it is a full-time job just growing enough food to feed the family.

KEY FACTS

● In Uganda's rural areas, only 42% of the population has access to health services, compared with 99% in urban areas.
● In 1994, the number of people per doctor in Uganda was 26,850 – over 60 times more people than in the UK or USA.
● The average daily calorie supply in Tanzania is 2,100 (about 95% of recommended levels), while in the USA and UK it is over 3,300 (30% more than needed).

RULE AND LAW

Kenya, Tanzania and Uganda have existed as independent countries only since the 1960s. Until then, they were European colonies, with the British controlling all three after 1918. Before that date, mainland Tanzania was a German colony known as German East Africa. The British gained control after the German defeat in the First World War. The territory was renamed Tanganyika, and it remained

under British control until 1961, when it peacefully gained independence under the leadership of Julius Nyerere. In 1964, Tanganyika united with the British-controlled island of Zanzibar and the new country was named Tanzania.

Julius Nyerere believed in SOCIALISM and launched an experimental programme of UJAMAA villages where rural people would live and work collectively to develop the country's agriculture. In 1967, he confirmed his socialist stance in a widespread NATIONALIZATION programme proclaimed in the Arusha Declaration, a significant event in African political history. During the 1970s, socialist development continued and rural people were firstly persuaded, and later forced, to move into large collective villages. This process of 'villagization'

▲ *Julius Nyerere became the first President of independent Tanzania in 1964. He pursued a socialist development path.*

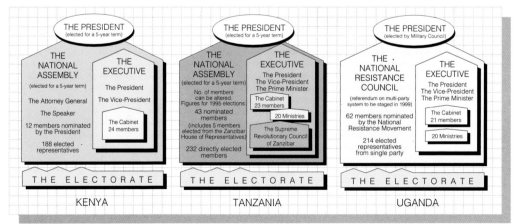

involved moving more than 2.5 million people into over 5,000 settlements, with the aim of increasing agricultural productivity and improving standards of living. It is generally agreed that villagization failed, and by the 1980s Tanzania had started to move away from its socialist path.

Kenya was the scene of a violent independence struggle led by an African rebel group, the Mau Mau, who terrorized British settlers and their supporters in an attempt to drive them out of the country. Between 1952 and 1956, 100 Europeans and around 2,000 of their African sympathizers were killed by the Mau Mau. Government forces killed about 12,000 Mau Mau rebels, mostly from the Kikuyu tribe who dominated the movement.

Many African people were held in detention centres during the troubles, and suspected leaders were arrested, including Jomo Kenyatta, who later became Kenya's

▼ *Dignitaries, including Jomo Kenyatta, gather for Kenya's independence day celebrations in 1963.*

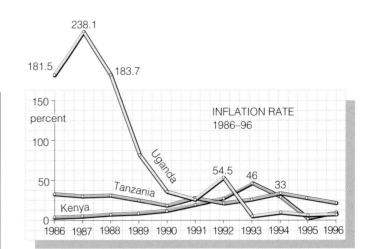

INFLATION RATE
1986–96

KEY FACTS

● Between 1980 and 1994, the amount of official development aid received by East Africa more than doubled.

● In 1994, Uganda's armed forces had 50,000 troops – more than double the number of troops it had in 1984.

● During the years of instability in Uganda, an estimated 500,000 people lost their lives, most of them when Idi Amin was in power.

● Kenya has 78 prisons designed to hold 21,000 prisoners, but by July 1995 they housed nearly 50,000.

● In November 1995, Benjamin Mkapa became President of Tanzania after winning the country's first elections to be contested by different political parties.

first President. Although the Mau Mau failed in their rebellion, the British government lost confidence in its ability to control the country and promised independence to Kenya, which finally came in 1963.

As Kenya's President, Jomo Kenyatta set about building a strong, stable economy. He died in 1978 and was succeeded by Daniel arap Moi, who continued to build

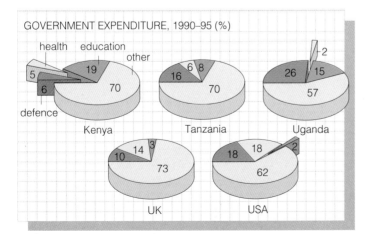

GOVERNMENT EXPENDITURE, 1990–95 (%)

▲ *Daniel arap Moi being sworn in as the new President of Kenya in 1978.*

the economy. Moi was reluctant to accept criticism of his policies, and has more or less eliminated opposition parties in Kenya.

Uganda became independent in 1962 under Milton Obote. Almost immediately, the country entered a period of violence and turmoil as competition erupted between the country's system of tribal kingdoms.

▲ *A stockpile of poached ivory is torched in Kenya's Nairobi National Park. President Moi has introduced tough laws to protect Kenya's wildlife from poachers.*

Obote exiled the most powerful leaders (kabakas), strengthening his control, but this led to economic collapse and allegations of corruption. In 1971, Obote's military leader, Idi Amin, staged a military coup and took control of the country.

Over the next eight years, Idi Amin conducted a reign of terror in Uganda, banning opposition parties, torturing people who spoke out against him, wiping out opposing tribal groups, and expelling the entire Asian population of around 65,000 people. In 1978, Amin's army attacked Tanzania, but Nyerere massed his troops and drove Amin back into Uganda, eventually forcing him to flee the country.

With Amin ousted and Nyerere's troops maintaining a fragile peace, Uganda set about rebuilding its tattered nation and Obote came to power again in 1980. When Tanzanian troops withdrew in 1982, political chaos and violence returned, leading to a second military coup in 1986. The new military President, Yoweri Museveni, has brought relative stability and peace to Uganda. The rebuilding of the economy and INFRASTRUCTURE provides great hope for the future of the country.

FOOD AND FARMING

CASH CROPS

Farming is the main activity in East Africa, employing more than 80% of the population. Most of the region's major commodities are based on agriculture and for some products the region is a major world producer. For example, Uganda is the world's fifth largest coffee producer and Kenya is fourth in world production of tea. The islands of Pemba and Zanzibar off the coast of Tanzania are even more significant. They are the world's biggest producers of cloves, a spice used in cooking.

All these crops are known as 'cash crops', which means they are grown mainly for

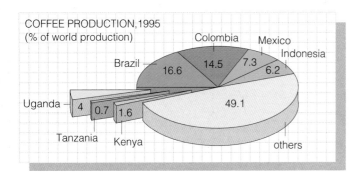

COFFEE PRODUCTION, 1995
(% of world production)

- Colombia 14.5
- Mexico 7.3
- Indonesia 6.2
- Brazil 16.6
- Uganda 4
- Tanzania 0.7
- Kenya 1.6
- others 49.1

▲ *Pemba and Zanzibar are the world's biggest producers of cloves. When they have been picked, the cloves are spread out on large mats to dry in the sun.*

▲ *Coffee beans are picked from bushes before being taken for drying and processing. East Africa is one of the world's major coffee producers.*

selling on the world markets rather than for consumption by local people. Cash crops are normally worth more money than local crops, but there is always the risk that prices will fall because of changing world demands. For that reason, it is a good idea for farmers to grow several different crops, so that if the price of one crop falls they still have another to sell. Another reason for growing several crops is to reduce the impact of drought, disease or pests which can devastate one crop, but leave another untouched.

SUBSISTENCE FARMING

Although agriculture is an important industry, providing employment for thousands of people and earning valuable foreign exchange for the economy, most farmers use at least half of their land to grow food for their families or for sale in local markets. The type of crops grown varies greatly throughout the region, depending on soil, rainfall and temperature conditions. African farmers are very skilled and understand their local environment at least as well as the best-trained scientists, and in many cases their knowledge is much greater. By growing crops with different

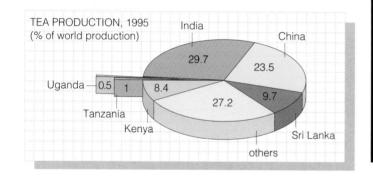

TEA PRODUCTION, 1995
(% of world production)

India 29.7
China 23.5
Sri Lanka 9.7
others 27.2
Kenya 8.4
Tanzania 1
Uganda 0.5

KEY FACTS

● In 1995–96, Uganda produced 4.1 million bags of coffee (the most for 20 years), but low prices meant earnings fell to US$ 388.9 million, down from US$ 432.6 million the previous season.

● With a total area of just 980 square kilometres, Pemba has over 3 million clove trees – more than 3,000 per square kilometre.

● In Tanzania, about 20% of the land has over 750 mm of rain a year (the minimum needed for cultivation), but only 8% is actually cultivated.

● East Africa's agricultural labour force declined by 8% between 1960 and 1990, compared with falls of 21% in Bangladesh, 27% in Mexico and 47% in Botswana.

● Between 1981 and 1993, food production per person fell by around 20% in Kenya and Tanzania, but grew by nearly 10% in Uganda.

water needs, such as cassava which needs very little water compared with maize, they can ensure that they will have some food even if the rains are poor.

Most farmers grow some crops known as 'staple crops'. These are items that form the basis of their diet, such as wheat and potatoes in the UK and USA, or rice in much of Asia. In East Africa, the staple crops are maize, millet, sorghum, cassava and MATOKE. A matoke looks like a banana,

◀ *Kenya is a major producer of tea. When ready, the green leaves are picked by thousands of workers and carried in large baskets to the estate factory, where they are processed.*

LABOUR FORCE, 1990 (%)

Kenya
- agriculture 80
- services 13
- industry 7

Tanzania
- 84
- 11
- 5

Uganda
- 84
- 11
- 5

China
- 72
- 13
- 15

Singapore
- 36
- 64

UK
- 29
- 69
- 2
- no agriculture

USA
- 26
- 71
- 3

▼ *Fishing has become a key part of the economy around Lake Victoria.*

but has a savoury taste and is boiled before it is eaten. It belongs to a group of plants called plantains that are also eaten by people in parts of South America and Asia.

In addition to staple crops, farmers also grow vegetables such as chillies, tomatoes and beans, and various fruits including mangoes, bananas and pawpaws. At first sight, many fields look very disorganized, but a closer look shows how the farmer plants several different crops on the same piece of land. This is a technique known as 'intercropping', which ensures a regular supply of food throughout the year as the various crops are planted and harvested at different times.

People also eat meat from chickens, sheep and goats, and use milk from cattle. Cattle are very important to African farmers.

To many pastoral groups, they are seen as a symbol of wealth. The Maasai are one such group, who live mainly by herding their cattle and exchanging milk for meat and vegetables. The Maasai have a traditional drink which is made of cow's milk that is mixed with fresh blood taken from a vein in the cow's neck.

FISHING

People living around Lake Victoria and other freshwater lakes supplement their diet with fish. In recent years, fishing has increased dramatically to become an important part of the local economy. Traditionally, the main fish caught in Lake Victoria were tilapia, similar to carp, and a small sardine-like fish called omena. However, during the 1950s the British

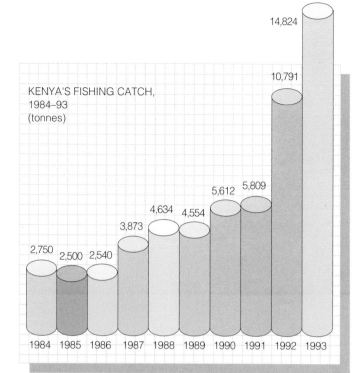

KENYA'S FISHING CATCH,
1984–93
(tonnes)

14,824

10,791

5,612 5,809

4,634 4,554

3,873

2,750 2,500 2,540

1984 1985 1986 1987 1988 1989 1990 1991 1992 1993

introduced a fish called the Nile perch, which has permanently changed the nature of the lake.

The Nile perch, which can weigh as much as a small adult, is a predator and has eaten many of the other fish in Lake Victoria. It was introduced for eating and today accounts for a large proportion of the fish catch. The Nile perch is popular outside Africa, and there are several factories that package it to sell in European and Israeli supermarkets.

In the past few years, the intensive fishing activity on Lake Victoria has meant that many fish are caught before they reach breeding age, so there is a risk that catches will begin to fall in the near future. There is also a problem with a weed called water hyacinth that has spread over large

◀ *The Nile perch is an introduced species that has boosted the local economy, but it has also eaten many of the traditional freshwater species.*

KEY FACTS

● The Maasai graze more than 100,000 cattle in Tanzania's Ngorongoro Crater, which they share with approximately 30,000 wild animals.
● Kenya's fishing catch increased by over 500% between 1984 and 1993, reaching a total of 14,824 tonnes.
● In 1995, Kenya's horticulture industry earned 10.6 billion Kenyan shillings (US$ 207 million) – up from 3.2 billion in 1990.
● Together with Zambia and Zimbabwe, Kenya, Tanzania and Uganda produce over 900 million roses a year.

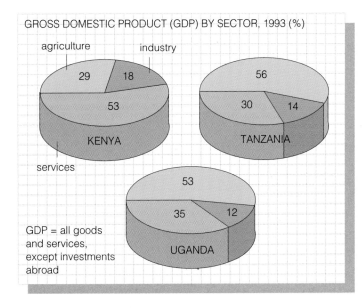

GROSS DOMESTIC PRODUCT (GDP) BY SECTOR, 1993 (%)

agriculture   industry

29   18

53

KENYA

services

56

30   14

TANZANIA

53

35   12

UGANDA

GDP = all goods
and services,
except investments
abroad

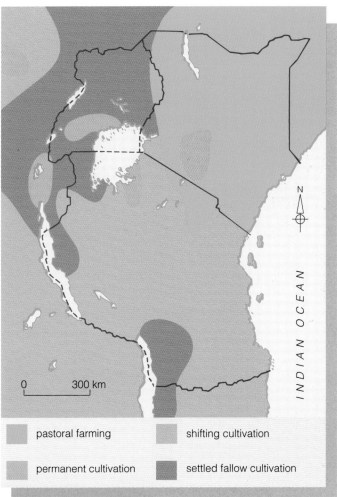

pastoral farming

permanent cultivation

shifting cultivation

settled fallow cultivation

N

INDIAN OCEAN

0   300 km

sections of the lake, making it difficult for fishermen to pull up their nets and get their boats to shore.

HORTICULTURE

The most recent development in the region's farming is the growth of the horticultural industry during the 1980s. This involves the production of fresh fruit, vegetables and cut

◀ *These women in Zanzibar are grinding millet between two heavy stones to crush the grain into a flour. This is then used to make a type of porridge that is one of the staple foods in East Africa.*

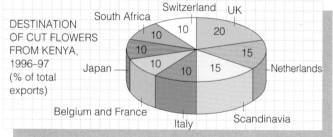

DESTINATION OF CUT FLOWERS FROM KENYA, 1996–97 (% of total exports)

South Africa 10
Switzerland 10
UK 20
Netherlands 15
Scandinavia 15
Italy 10
Belgium and France 10
Japan 10

▲ *Flowers are an important part of Kenya's flourishing horticulture industry. They are grown in specially controlled greenhouses – such as here, in Thika – and then exported all over the world.*

flowers for sale in European, Asian and Middle Eastern markets. Products include mangoes, melons, green beans, mangetout, avocados, and flowers such as roses, chrysanthemums and lilies.

The industry employs thousands of people and is growing very quickly to satisfy European demand for fresh food and flowers throughout the year. So far, smaller farmers have not benefited from this new market, because they cannot compete with the big producers. In Kenya, small farmers are beginning to organize themselves into co-operative groups so that they can compete effectively, but it is not yet clear how well this will work.

TRADE AND INDUSTRY

East Africa's industrial sector is very small compared with African economies such as South Africa, Zimbabwe and Nigeria. There are petroleum refineries at Mombasa in Kenya, while Uganda and Kenya have some metal processing and car plants, but they employ few people and contribute relatively little to the economy.

Tourism is an important industry throughout the region. In Kenya, where it is most developed, it is one of the biggest earners of foreign exchange. Tourists are attracted by the region's fantastic landscape, abundant wildlife and friendly people. Tanzania has the best opportunity to develop its tourist industry because of its enormous national parks. The Selous Game Reserve in the south of the country is the largest in the world, covering an area of 50,000 square kilometres – nearly twice the size of neighbouring Rwanda and bigger than Switzerland.

One rapidly growing industry is the processing of agricultural products such as tea, coffee, vegetables and fruit. As the demand for these goods increases on the world markets, this sector should continue to expand. It is an important industry, as it is more profitable for countries to process their own goods rather than to export them in a raw state.

East Africa's main trading partners are European, with the UK, Germany and Spain particularly important. Other key partners include Japan and India.

Kenya, Tanzania and Uganda are striving to establish a regional co-operation for trade, to be called East African Co-operation (EAC).

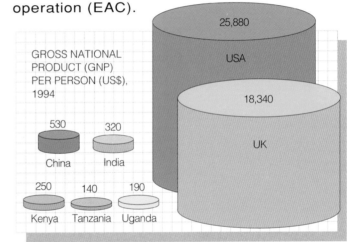

GROSS NATIONAL PRODUCT (GNP) PER PERSON (US$), 1994

25,880 USA

18,340 UK

530 China

320 India

250 Kenya

140 Tanzania

190 Uganda

◄ *Tourism is very important in East Africa, creating jobs and an income for many local people. Here in Maasai Mara, tourists are watching the lions – or is it the other way round?*

◄ *Processing food such as pineapples has become an important industry in East Africa.*

▼ *Here, German cars are being built under licence by workers at a plant in Thika, Kenya.*

This would be similar to the European Union (EU) or the North American Free Trade Agreement (NAFTA), allowing for privileged trading arrangements between the member countries, such as the lifting of import and export duties.

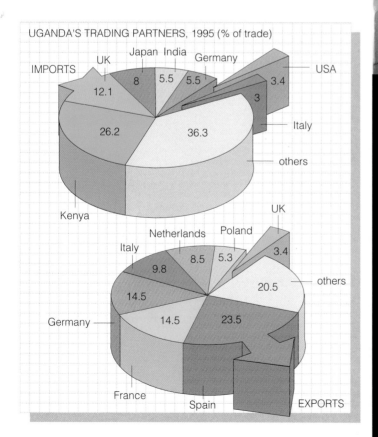

UGANDA'S TRADING PARTNERS, 1995 (% of trade)

IMPORTS

UK 12.1
Japan 8
India 5.5
Germany 5.5
USA 3.4
Italy 3
others 36.3
Kenya 26.2

EXPORTS

Netherlands 8.5
Poland 5.3
UK 3.4
others 20.5
Italy 9.8
Germany 14.5
France 14.5
Spain 23.5

KEY FACTS

● In the USA, GROSS NATIONAL PRODUCT per person is around 100 times greater than in Kenya and almost 185 times greater than in Tanzania.

● The number of visitors to Kenya rose from 362,000 in 1980 to 676,000 in 1994, but fell below 500,000 in 1996. Most travelled from Germany and the UK.

● In Kenya, earnings from processing horticultural produce rose dramatically from 1.52 billion Kenyan shillings in 1990 to 3.33 billion in 1994 (about US$ 64 million).

TRANSPORT

East Africa's transport system is not at all developed compared with those of Europe or North America, but for Africa it is relatively good. Paved roads connect the main centres, but many are in a poor condition and are more like dirt tracks. Few people own cars, so most people use buses or the brightly coloured minibuses known as matatus to travel by road.

The main regional railway was built by the British and runs from Mombasa to Kasese, near Uganda's border with Zaire. Nairobi, now the region's main city, began life as a storage depot for the railway's construction workers. Tanzania has a separate rail network, built by the Germans and extended by the British. It spreads westwards from Dar es Salaam in a fan shape, with one line, built by the Chinese in the 1960s, continuing into Zambia. Travel by rail is very slow, and there is often only one train a day between main centres.

Lake Victoria is important for the region's transport, and ferries operate both local and international routes. Most are open-decked and very crowded, carrying everything from

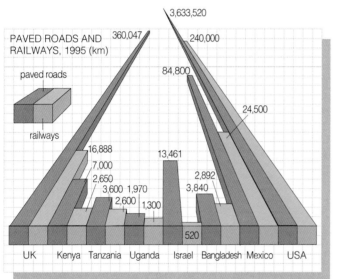

PAVED ROADS AND RAILWAYS, 1995 (km)

paved roads

railways

	UK	Kenya	Tanzania	Uganda	Israel	Bangladesh	Mexico	USA
paved roads	360,047	16,888	3,600	2,600	13,461	3,840	84,800	3,633,520
railways		7,000	2,650	1,970	1,300	2,892	240,000	24,500
					520			

◄ *Open-decked ferries operating on Lake Victoria are an important form of transport for trade and travel between all three countries in the region.*

lorries and buses to people taking their goats or chickens to market.

Nairobi is a major air TRANSPORT-HUB and the volume of traffic is increasing rapidly. There are several flights a day between the region's main cities and several new airports are planned to accommodate the increase in international traffic.

The Indian Ocean ports of Mombasa and Dar es Salaam are two of the busiest in Africa. They are very important for trade with Europe, the Middle East and India and serve many of Africa's land-locked states, with freight being transferred by road or railway.

However, for many people in the region, walking, or possibly cycling, is the main means of travelling. It is not unusual for people to walk more than 30 kilometres to reach a market or place of work.

▶ **Crowded buses cover most of the main routes between towns.**

▲ *Air travel is the easiest way to cover the large distances between the region's main centres, or to reach parks and reserves such as the Maasai Mara.*

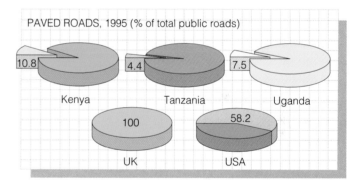

PAVED ROADS, 1995 (% of total public roads)

Kenya	Tanzania	Uganda
10.8	4.4	7.5

UK	USA
100	58.2

THE ENVIRONMENT

◀ *The savanna area is sparsely populated by pastoral people. They regularly move their grazing livestock to avoid damaging the environment.*

The region has a rich and varied natural environment. The rainforests of western Uganda are the last in East Africa and are home to about 300 mountain gorillas — about half the total world population of this highly endangered species. The savanna plains that cover southern Kenya and most of Tanzania contain a fantastic variety of large mammal wildlife, including elephants, giraffes, zebras, lions, wildebeest and many species of antelope. This area is almost uninhabited by humans, apart from a few pastoral communities. The great lakes of the region, such as Lakes Victoria, Turkana and Tanganyika, provide another important environment, while the soda lakes of the Rift Valley have a very rare ecology that is found in only a few places on earth.

However, East Africa does have environmental problems. Its rapidly growing population has created much pressure on the environment and in some areas there is now great cause for concern. The region's main problems are water shortages, deforestation, soil erosion and desertificaton. These difficulties are frequently related, so that one leads to another, or increases the chances of another problem occurring.

Traffic and waste pollution are problems in urban areas, and in some of the shanty towns they present a serious health hazard. The shortage of safe water and adequate sanitation facilities is one of the region's biggest problems, especially in overcrowded city slums. People are often forced to drink water that may have been used for washing, cleaning clothes and watering livestock. Many of the region's major diseases, such as hepatitis, typhoid, dysentery and diarrhoea, are transmitted by

▼ *Not all of East Africa's environmental problems are caused by people. Heavy storms during the rains can cause massive soil erosion, or 'gullying'.*

KEY FACTS

● In 1994, nationally protected areas covered 14.7% of Tanzania's total land, 8.1% of Uganda's and 6% of Kenya's.

● In the 1960s, the Maasai protested at the loss of their grazing lands by killing rhinos and elephants in Amboseli National Park, southern Kenya.

● Since Kenya introduced an ivory ban in 1989, the number of elephants poached has fallen from 5,000 a year to 50–60 a year. The elephant population has increased by about 1,000 every year.

them rely on the land, plants and animals for their livelihood. Governments also know that the environment is important for the tourist industry and have set up more than 97 nationally protected areas to preserve the region's landscapes and wildlife. Some 139,000 square kilometres of Tanzania's total area are set aside as protected areas, including Selous Game Reserve, the largest reserve in the world. In Kenya's Nakuru National Park, black rhinos are heavily protected behind electric fences patrolled by armed guards. This is because poaching reduced Kenya's rhino population from about 20,000 in 1970 to less than 500 by the late 1980s. But this type of protection can disrupt local people's lives, sometimes

using dirty water, so infection rates are often very high in crowded slum areas. Many rural areas also lack safe water and sanitation facilities, so people have to use the nearest stream, river or lake to meet their requirements.

The East African people are very aware of their environment because so many of

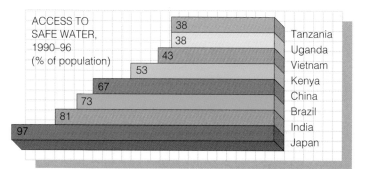

ACCESS TO SAFE WATER, 1990–96 (% of population)

38	Tanzania
38	Uganda
43	Vietnam
53	Kenya
67	China
73	Brazil
81	India
97	Japan

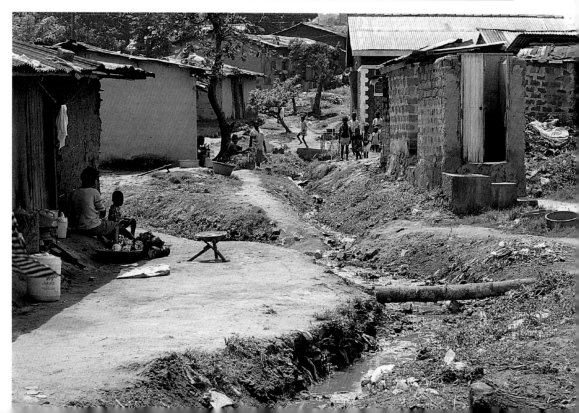

► *Lack of safe water and sanitation facilities means that urban slums – such as this one in Kampala, Uganda – are often plagued with disease problems. One major hazard is malaria. It is transmitted by mosquitoes, which breed in shallow pools and streams.*

causing conflict. The Maasai, who traditionally used park lands for collecting food, grazing livestock and hunting game, have been severely affected by the setting up of national parks in Kenya.

In many parts of East Africa, local people and the government or overseas agencies work together on local small-scale schemes to protect the environment. Projects include tree-planting schemes to replace trees cut down for fuelwood. The tree roots also bind the soil, so reducing soil erosion, while planting fruit trees can provide food for local people to eat or to sell. Other tree

▼ *The region's rhino population is protected in special reserves. This is the area around Ngorongoro Crater, Tanzania.*

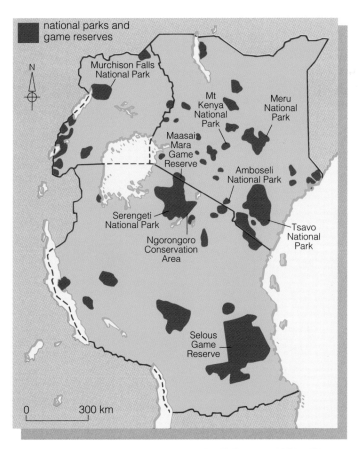

national parks and game reserves

N

Murchison Falls National Park

Mt Kenya National Park

Meru National Park

Maasai Mara Game Reserve

Amboseli National Park

Serengeti National Park

Ngorongoro Conservation Area

Tsavo National Park

Selous Game Reserve

0   300 km

species can provide fodder for animals, fuelwood and building materials, or can act as a fertilizer, according to the farmers' needs. This multiple use of trees is known as 'agroforestry', a combination of agriculture and forestry, and is considered very important for East Africa's future environmental protection.

Other local schemes, such as in Machakos District, near Nairobi in Kenya, include TERRACING on slopes to prevent soil erosion, building small dams in order to catch and store rainwater, and improved crop management.

▶ *In dry rural areas such as northern Kenya, people may have to dig deep holes in order to reach water.*

◀ *Tree nurseries are often organized by local people, with money from the government or other agencies. Later, the trees will be planted elsewhere to protect the soil and to provide fuelwood, fruit and other resources. It is especially common for women's groups to be involved in these projects – such as this one in Meru, Kenya.*

THE FUTURE

East Africa is entering a period of new challenges and fresh opportunities. The plans for a new East African Co-operation will reinforce the area's political and economic stability and allow it to compete with the southern African states that have emerged as Africa's major economic region since the mid-1990s. Kenya's important tourist industry has already lost up to 20% of its visitors to South Africa and Zimbabwe, and competition is likely to increase in the agricultural sector too. Horticultural production has great potential to strengthen the East African economies, especially as land is plentiful. It can also lead to other industries, such as processing and packaging, which increase export income and provide more jobs.

Any future developments in East Africa must be able to support the rapidly growing population for many years without harming the environment on which so many people rely. Projects such as tree nurseries, soil protection and water management must be encouraged through rural development schemes that also provide basic services such as education and health. These schemes make rural living more attractive and encourage people to remain in the villages, rather than migrating to already overcrowded urban centres.

East Africa's most important challenges for the future are to maintain peace and stability, to promote regional co-operation and to meet the basic needs of its people. Achieving these aims will allow its population to develop the skills necessary to take East Africa into the 21st century as a centre of power on the African continent.

KEY FACTS

● In 1996, Kenya's government and the World Bank launched a US$ 165 million programme to upgrade and maintain the country's road network.

● During 1996, new gold reserves were discovered around the southern shores of Lake Victoria in Tanzania. Production is expected to start in 1999.

● The East African Co-operation (EAC) is due to expand into a Common Market for Eastern and Southern Africa (COMESA) by the year 2000.

▲ *Co-operative projects, such as this soil and water management scheme in Kenya, are important for maintaining rural development.*

▶ *Tourists are increasingly looking for adventure holidays in remote areas. This is a potential key industry for East Africa.*

FURTHER INFORMATION

● KENYAN HIGH COMMISSION
(EDUCATION DEPARTMENT)
45 Portland Place, London W1N 4AS
Provides education packs on Kenya.
● KENYAN TOURIST OFFICE
25 Brooks Mews, London W1Y 1LF
*Provides posters, leaflets and general
information on Kenya.*
● TANZANIAN HIGH COMMISSION
43 Hertford Street, London W1Y 8DB
Provides general information on Tanzania.
● UGANDAN HIGH COMMISSION
Uganda House, 58/59 Trafalgar Square,
London WC2N 5DX
Provides general information on Uganda.

BOOKS ABOUT THE REGION
● *Continents: Africa*, Colm Regan and Peter
Cremin, Wayland 1996 (age 10+)
● *Country Insights: Kenya*, Máiréad Dunne.
Wambui Kairi and Eric Nyamjon, Wayland
1997 (age 8–10)
● *Kenya: A Geography Resource Pack*, Nick
Reggler, Worldaware 1995 (age 12–14)
● *Africa: Eyewitness Guides*, Yvonne Ayo,
Dorling Kindersley 1995 (age 10+)
● *Land, Environment and Pastoralism in
Kenya*, Leeds Development Education
Centre 1993 (age 12+)

GLOSSARY

CASH CROPS
Crops which are grown mainly for sale in overseas markets, but can also be sold in local markets.

DESERTIFICATION
The process whereby a piece of land becomes barren and infertile — like a desert. This can be caused by deforestation, over-cultivation and soil erosion. It is very difficult to reverse.

GEOLOGICAL FAULT
A line of weakness in the earth's crust, caused by violent movement deep inside the earth over millions of years. Volcanoes and earthquakes are often associated with these areas.

GROSS NATIONAL PRODUCT (GNP)
The total value of all the goods and services produced by a country in a year.

INDEPENDENCE
The transfer of power from a foreign colonial country to a government set up by local people who are then able to control their own affairs.

INFORMAL SECTOR
Although usually not officially recognized, this involves people selling various goods or offering different services, generally in the streets or in markets.

INFRASTRUCTURE
A network for transmitting and transporting such things as water, electricity, information or vehicles. Examples are electricity pylons and motorways/expressways.

MATATUS
Minibuses used in East Africa to transport people and their goods. They are often brightly coloured and the driver plays loud music.

MATOKE
A savoury banana eaten as a staple food in Uganda. The matoke (or plantain, as it is known elsewhere) is peeled and boiled before it is eaten.

NATIONALIZATION
The process of government taking control of major industries, transport networks and financial institutions. This is the opposite of privatization and is normally associated with socialist governments.

NOMADIC
A lifestyle where people move from place to place — usually involving livestock herders moving with their animals in search of pasture and water.

PASTORALISTS
People who make their living by herding animals. The Maasai are an example of a pastoral community.

SAVANNA
A tropical vegetation consisting of grasses, shrubs and scattered trees. It is typically dry for most of the year, but bursts into life when the first rains arrive.

SEMI-ARID
A halfway zone between savanna grassland and desert. Vegetation is typically sparse, due to lack of rainfall.

SOCIALISM
A system of government that is based on equality for the people. It works on the idea that resources and profits are shared, rather than concentrated in the hands of certain individuals or small groups.

TERRACING
Cutting strips of farmland into the side of a hill, forming a pattern of 'steps'. This method reduces soil erosion.

TRANSPORT-HUB
The meeting or crossover point of major road, rail, sea and air transport routes, usually in large cities such as Dar es Salaam, Nairobi, London, New York and Tokyo.

UJAMAA
A Swahili word meaning 'familyhood'. In Tanzania, it refers to village settlements where people live and work together on agricultural projects.